Trade in our Global Community

Rachel Eagen

CRABTREE
PUBLISHING COMPANY
WWW.CRABTREEBOOKS.COM

Money $ense

An Introduction to Financial Literacy

Author: Rachel Eagen

Series research and development: Reagan Miller

Editors: Reagan Miller and Janine Deschenes

Design and photo research: Tammy McGarr

Proofreader: Petrice Custance

Prepress technician: Tammy McGarr

Print and production coordinator: Katherine Berti

Photographs
iStock: ©Jacob Wackerhausen, p 18

Shutterstock: ©chrisdorney, p 4 (bottom); ©WorldPictures, p 7 (top); ©Alf Ribeiro, p 8, ©VladSV, p 10, ©Wachiwit, p 13 (middle right); ©mikecphoto, p 15; ©Alexander Image. p 16; ©Denys Prykhodov, p 19;

All other images from Shutterstock

Library and Archives Canada Cataloguing in Publication

Eagen, Rachel, 1979-, author
        Trade in our global community / Rachel Eagen.

(Money sense : an introduction to financial literacy)
Includes index.
Issued in print and electronic formats.
ISBN 978-0-7787-5186-1 (hardcover).--
ISBN 978-0-7787-5188-5 (softcover).--
ISBN 978-1-4271-2138-7 (HTML)

        1. International trade--Juvenile literature. 2. Commerce--Juvenile
literature. 3. Exchange--Juvenile literature. I. Title.

HF1379.E24 2018   j382   C2018-902970-6
                                                                          C2018-902971-4

Library of Congress Cataloging-in-Publication Data

Names: Eagen, Rachel, 1979- author.
Title: Trade in our global community / Rachel Eagen.
Description: New York : Crabtree Publishing Company, [2018] |
   Series: Money sense: An introduction to financial literacy | Includes index.
Identifiers: LCCN 2018025223 (print) | LCCN 2018028964 (ebook) |
   ISBN 9781427121387 (Electronic) |
   ISBN 9780778751861 (hardcover) |
   ISBN 9780778751885 (pbk.)
Subjects: LCSH: International trade--Juvenile literature. |
   Commercial policy--Juvenile literature.
Classification: LCC HF1379 (ebook) | LCC HF1379 .E24 2018 (print) |
   DDC 382--dc23
LC record available at https://lccn.loc.gov/2018025223

Crabtree Publishing Company

www.crabtreebooks.com   1-800-387-7650

Printed in the U.S.A./092018/CG20180719

Published in Canada
Crabtree Publishing
616 Welland Ave.
St. Catharines, Ontario
L2M 5V6

Published in the United States
Crabtree Publishing
PMB 59051
350 Fifth Avenue, 59th Floor
New York, New York 10118

Published in the United Kingdom
Crabtree Publishing
Maritime House
Basin Road North, Hove
BN41 1WR

Published in Australia
Crabtree Publishing
3 Charles Street
Coburg North
VIC 3058

Table of Contents

Hi, I'm Ava and this is Finn. Get ready for an inside look on spending, saving, and more! The *Money Sense* series explores smart ways to think about and manage money.

After reading this book, join us online at Crabtree Plus to learn more and solve problems. Just use the Digital Code on page 22 in this book.

Meeting Needs and Wants

Every person has needs and wants. A need is something that you must have to survive, such as food and shelter. A want is something that you would like to have, such as a new video game. We buy **goods** and **services** to meet our needs and wants.

A service is something a person does for someone else, such as cleaning their teeth.

A good is something you can touch, such as a chocolate bar.

Producers and Consumers

Goods and services come from **producers**. They make the goods and provide the services you use to meet your needs and wants. When you use goods or services, you are a **consumer**. Everyone is a consumer, because everyone must buy goods and services to meet their wants and needs.

Consumers and producers in a community depend on each other. Consumers need producers to provide goods and services. Producers need consumers to buy them.

Our Global Community

Together, the people who live on planet Earth share a **global community**. Producers and consumers in the global community depend on each other. Consumers buy goods and services from producers in different parts of the world. This is called global **trade**.

Trade connects communities and countries around the world.

Cars, aircraft, and medicine are some of the goods sent from the United States to other parts of the world.

Trade is Global

One country cannot produce all of the goods and services needed to meet the wants and needs of the people who live there. Countries bring in goods and services from other countries. Countries also send goods and services to other countries that need them.

Pineapples, rice, and some electronics are goods that come into the United States from other countries.

Goods in Different Countries

Coffee beans are grown and collected by farmers in countries with warm climates, such as Brazil.

Countries produce different types of goods. The types of goods that a country produces usually depends on its **climate** or its location on Earth. Some types of foods, such as coffee, are grown only in warm climates. Goods such as gold only come from countries where they can be **mined** from the ground.

Canada

Meeting Needs Around the World

Countries trade goods with each other to meet the wants and needs of the people who live there. They **export**, or send out, goods they can produce themselves, and **import**, or bring in, goods they cannot produce themselves.

Florida oranges

Oranges are grown in Florida, where it is warm. Countries that have cooler climates, such as Canada, import Florida oranges because oranges cannot be grown there.

Make "**cents**" of it!

Take a trip to the grocery store with an adult and look for signs that tell you where the fruits and vegetables came from. Which fruits and vegetables were grown in your country? From which countries were fruits and vegetables imported?

9

Goods in Your Country

Every day, you use goods made in other countries. You also use goods that are produced in your country. These are called **domestic goods**. These goods sometimes stay in your country to be sold to consumers there. Other times, they are sent to other countries.

Giant trains, trucks, and ships bring American domestic goods, such as cars, to other countries all over the world.

Government Goods and Services

Governments in different countries make goods and provide services for the people who live there. Government services usually help people have better lives. For example, most governments provide health care services. Governments also provide goods, such as library books and school supplies, that all people in a country can use.

Street lights are goods that are often provided by a country's government.

Mail delivery is a service that is provided by most governments.

11

A Global Market

A market is any place where goods and services are traded, or bought and sold. Your community is a **local** market because goods and services are bought and sold there. All of the countries and people on Earth are part of a **global market**, too.

The global market is all of the trade that happens between people and countries on Earth.

We Need Trade

Today, there are many goods and services available to consumers. At the grocery store, we can buy rice from Asia and chocolate from Africa. We can go to the mall and buy clothing made in Vietnam, or cell phones made in China. Without the global market, we would not have so many choices!

Supply and Demand

There is not an unlimited number of goods and services in the global market. The amount of a good or service that is available to buy is called the **supply**. The number of people who want to buy a good or service is the **demand**. Producers try to provide the right number of goods and services to meet the demand of consumers.

After a strong growing season, there is a high supply of oranges. If many consumers want to buy oranges, the supply can meet the demand.

Countries trade goods such as lumber with each other to help make sure the supply can meet the demand.

Meeting the Demand

Countries import goods with a low supply and high demand. They export goods with a high supply and low demand. Canada produces a lot of **lumber**. The demand for lumber in Canada is not high enough to use all of it. Canada exports the lumber to countries where there is a low supply. These countries buy the lumber to meet the demand there.

Scarcity in the Global Market

Scarcity happens when there are not enough goods and services produced to meet everyone's wants and needs. Gold is a good that is scarce because although many people want it, there is not a lot of it. Doctors provide health care services that many people need, but there is a limited number of doctors.

Some goods become scarce during certain times. Foods that only grow in summer are scarce in winter. Some toys can be scarce before Christmas!

Scarcity and Price

How much money something costs is related to scarcity. Usually, the more scarce a good or service is, the higher its **price**. This is because many people want it, but it is harder to get. Countries do not have unlimited money to spend on importing goods and services. They have to choose which ones they can **afford** to import.

Gold has a high price because it is scarce. Countries that export gold can make a lot of money when other countries buy it.

FINE
GOLD
999.9

NET WT
1000g

Making Choices

There are many products and services in local and global markets for consumers to choose from. But consumers do not have an unlimited amount of money to buy all of the goods and services people want. So, they must choose to buy some things and give up others.

Consumers can make choices about whether to buy a domestic good or an imported good. Sometimes domestic and imported goods have different prices.

What to Buy?

Supply, demand, and scarcity are related to the buying choices that consumers make. When a good or service is scarce, or when it has a low supply and a high demand, it costs more money. People might need to choose to buy something that costs less money and is less scarce.

There is a high demand for **smartphones** in the global market. They also have a high price!

Make "**cents**" of it!

Do you have any birthday money, an allowance, or a piggy bank? Count up how much money you have. Next, make a list of three goods or services you would like to have. Do you have enough money to buy them? If not, how will you choose which ones to buy?

We Are All Connected

In the past, people ate the food, wore the clothing, and played with the toys they could produce themselves or buy from other people in their local community. Today, global trade means that we can buy almost anything we want and need—from anywhere in the world. We are all connected by global trade!

Do you like to eat foods from other countries? Global trade makes this possible!

Make "**cents**" of it!

Take a look at the label on the shirt you're wearing. You may need the help of a friend or adult to find it. Where was your shirt made? Write down the name of the country, then find it on a map. Compare your findings with your classmates.

Can you think of any other goods you have that come from other countries?

People around the world are connected by global trade. By using goods that came from places around the world, you are connected to the producers there!

Learning More

Books

Boelts, Maribeth. *Those Shoes*. Candlewick Press, 2007.

Loewen, Nancy. *Lemons and Lemonade: A Book About Supply and Demand*. Capstone, 2005.

Yonezu, Yusuke. *A Cup for Everyone*. Minedition, 2008.

Websites

Visit this site to watch a video clip about a group of kids who realize they depend on global trade.
http://bizkids.com/clip/global-marketplace-overview

Read more about producers and consumers and how a bicycle is produced at Kidsville News.
http://kidsvillenews.com/2014/12/kids/consumersproducers/

For fun challenges, activities, and more, enter the code at the Crabtree Plus website below.

www.crabtreeplus.com/money-sense

Your code is:
ms06

Words to Know

Note: Some **boldfaced** words are defined where they appear in the book.

afford (uh-FAWRD) verb To be able to buy something

climate (KLAHY-mit) noun The usual weather in a place

consumer (kuh n-SOO-mer) noun A person who buys and uses goods and services

export (ik-SPAWRT) verb To send out from one place, especially a country, to another

global community (GLOH-buh l kuh-MYOO-ni-tee) noun All of the people who live on planet Earth

governments (GUHV-ern-muh nts) noun The group of people who govern, or control, a country

import (im-PAWRT) verb To bring in from a different place, especially a country

lumber (LUHM-ber) noun Cut pieces of wood from trees that is used to build things

local (LOH-kuh l) adjective Belonging or related to a specific area, such as a neighborhood or town

mined (mahyn-ed) verb Dug up resources, such as gold, from under the ground

price (prahys) noun The amount of money that consumers pay for a good or service

producer (pruh-DOO-ser) noun A person who makes goods or provides services

trade (treyd) verb The exchange of goods and services. People can trade goods and services for other goods and services, or trade goods and services for money.

A noun is a person, place, or thing.

A verb is an action word that tells you what someone or something does.

An adjective is a word that tells you what something is like.

Index

About the Author

Rachel Eagen is a writer and editor. She spends most of her free time baking cookies, listening to music, playing ukulele, and going on adventures with her son. She once got lost in a local market in Morocco and never wanted to be found.